W9-BJZ-084

PAMPHLETS ON AMERICAN WRITERS · NUMBER 72

UNIVERSITY OF MINNESOTA

Mary McCarthy

BY IRVIN STOCK

812.
52
McCARTHY
Sto

FINKELSTEIN
MEMORIAL LIBRARY
SPRING VALLEY, N. Y.

UNIVERSITY OF MINNESOTA PRESS · MINNEAPOLIS

860645 PAPER

© Copyright 1968 by the University of Minnesota

ALL RIGHTS RESERVED

Printed in the United States of America at
the North Central Publishing Co., St. Paul

Library of Congress Catalog Card Number: 68-64755

PUBLISHED IN GREAT BRITAIN, INDIA, AND PAKISTAN BY THE OXFORD
UNIVERSITY PRESS, LONDON, BOMBAY, AND KARACHI, AND IN CANADA
BY THE COPP CLARK PUBLISHING CO. LIMITED, TORONTO

MARY McCARTHY

IRVIN STOCK, professor and chairman of the English department at the University of Massachusetts in Boston, is the author of *William Hale White (Mark Rutherford): A Critical Study* and has contributed articles on fiction to various literary quarterlies.

⤻ *Mary McCarthy*

MARY McCARTHY has so far written five novels, as well
as eight books of other kinds, and though all the novels are not
equally successful, each has so much life and truth, and is written
in a prose so spare, vigorous, and natural, and yet at the same
time so witty, graceful, and, in a certain way, poetic, that it becomes a matter for wonder that she is not generally named among
the finest American novelists of her period. She is much admired,
of course, and has achieved a best seller, but that is not the same
thing. The reason, I think, is that she is a sort of neoclassicist in
a country of romantics. The sprightliness and detachment of her
prose, her preference for sense over sensibility, her satirical eye
for the hidden ego in our intellectual pretensions are qualities
we are not comfortable with in this country. They may amuse,
but they also antagonize. And they don't, among all our heaven-
storming Titans, seem Important. At any rate, whatever the
reason, the qualities and meanings that lie beneath her sparkling
surface tend, even by admiring critics, to be misconceived. Her
novels have been called "essayistic," for instance — designed to per-
suade us of ideas rather than to present living characters and felt
experiences. And their subject is often supposed to be a supercili-
ous, zestfully destructive view of people she dislikes, a view unre-
deemed by any examples of the humanly admirable — except in
the heroines who represent herself. These charges are so common,
in fact, that it may be useful to begin with a preliminary answer to
each.

As to the first, though she has written mainly about her own class
of American intellectuals, people who try to live by ideas or to

give the appearance of doing so, and has therefore naturally admitted the play of ideas into her stories, her chief concerns have always been psychological, emotional, above all moral, the concerns of the novelist. Whenever her characters express ideas, something of more urgent human interest is also going on, whether they know it or not. And though her novels, like most of those which are nowadays taken seriously, are meaningfully organized, it is no simple polemical formula that turns out to be their meaning. It is rather the kind of vision, precisely the novelist's, which moves us, which enlarges our sympathies, and which brings us closer to a complex reality. The fact is, if one remembers her novels freshly at all, it is surely characters and not ideas which their titles bring first to mind — the man in the Brooks Brothers shirt, Macdougal Macdermott, Will Taub, Henry Mulcahy, Domna Rejnev, Miles Murphy, Warren Coe, the girls in "the group" and certain of their men and their parents. In novels these days, Miss McCarthy has complained, "there are hardly any people," only "sensibility" and "sensation," but her own have been an exception. Moreover, though she is of course right in noting the enormous difference between her art and that of the novelist she says she would most like to resemble, Tolstoy, yet her admiration for the godlike realist is reflected at least in the way her intentions are always buried deep inside a flesh of vividly rendered particulars. The concrete world of her people, their tics of behavior, their ways of talking — a precise notation of these gives her work throughout the special authority of the visible and the audible. Indeed, her eye for the particular qualities of things makes half the charm of her style, where it adds to the more sober virtues deriving from her intelligence and honesty a flashing witty poetry of metaphor.

As for that other notion, that she is a heartless satirist whose chief interest is to demonstrate her own superiority to the silliness of her victims — this is just as mistaken. While she does indeed

6

make characters out of people she regards as morally weak or ugly or dangerous, and makes them with a bold thrust toward grotesque extremes that recalls another writer she admires, Dickens, the norms of sense or decency which such people violate are equally vivid in her novels. We see these norms both in the passionate indignation between her lines and in the large number of her characters who cannot live without struggling toward them or becoming their champions. In fact, it is precisely one of her distinctions that she has succeeded in creating good people — even out of twentieth-century intellectuals! — who are at once convincing and attractive. It should be added, however, that the characters she values are not necessarily intellectuals. On the contrary, they may be, like Warren Coe, the kind of people at whom her clever, learned heroines tend to smile. And we must add also, what is equally true and equally unnoticed by the run of her critics, that the heroine who represents herself is often, for all her cleverness, the character most roughly treated by the ironical author. If she ends by coming out all right, it is with a rightness earned by much agonizing error, and itself riddled with imperfections sadly accepted.

Amid the currently fashionable criticism of fiction, a kind which concentrates so hard on technique or symbols that it often bypasses what technique and symbols are intended to serve, Miss McCarthy's ideas on the subject can be liberatingly sensible. Here (from "Settling the Colonel's Hash" in *On the Contrary*) is a remark that may be taken as an introduction to the present study:

It is now considered very old-fashioned and tasteless to speak of an author's "philosophy of life" as something that can be harvested from his work. Actually, most of the great authors did have a "philosophy of life" which they were eager to communicate to the public; this was one of their motives for writing. And to disentangle a moral philosophy from a work that evidently contains one is far less damaging to the author's purpose and the integrity of his art than to violate his imagery by symbol-hunting, as though reading a novel were a sort of paper-chase.

The images of a novel or a story belong, as it were, to a family, very closely knit and inseparable from each other; the parent "idea" of a story or a novel generates events and images all bearing a strong family resemblance. And to understand a story or a novel, you must look for the parent "idea," which is usually in plain view, if you read quite carefully and literally what the author says.

The same thing is surely true of the serious writer's total oeuvre: all his works will, for the same reason, show this family resemblance. Since Miss McCarthy, in spite of the abundant social reality in her novels, is as autobiographical a novelist as Fitzgerald or Hemingway, we can best approach the "parent idea" underlying her career by beginning with her life. And the first point to make is that it has been a life blessed — and cursed — with an unusual amount of freedom. Orphaned at six, she was taken care of for years by coldly cruel guardians and later by grandparents who were kind but detached. Doris Grumbach tells us that a former Vassar classmate, now a psychiatrist, remembers that at college Mary McCarthy was "'aloof, independent, irrelevant . . . lonely,' seemingly rootless because she, unlike most of the others, had no real family she had to please. 'She appeared to be much freer than we were and this fascinated and frightened us.'" Such freedom resembles, it is true, the freedom to think and do as they wish that many clever young people of our time claim as a right, but for the orphaned Mary McCarthy it was a condition more serious than a bright student's pose. She was really free, and had to experience what this meant in her deepest nature. And the kind of freedom that comes from having no family to please — is it not a freedom from those pressures, loyalties, urgencies of feeling that, though they hamper us, also give us a sense of who we are, of what is real, of what is right? To lack such direction can mean one is at the mercy of merely plausible ideas on such matters, ideas which decent people hope to choose according to their truth, of course, but which, amid the multiple "truths" life offers, even the best of us are in danger of choosing with our vanity, or our fear, or our lust. To be directed by external authority has its own dangers; these are the dangers of freedom.

Her work is about the painful mixed blessing of freedom for her kind of people — for intellectuals — and in particular, about how hard it has been for intellectuals in our time to behave decently and humanly. For to be free and clever has often meant only to be able to escape from difficult, limiting reality into the realm of flattering abstractions. And yet — for I have said that to speak of what she dislikes is to speak of only half her subject — if she shows what makes her kind go wrong, she shows just as vividly what makes them go right. She shows that sometimes, even in intellectuals free to please themselves, there arises a love for reality that is greater than love of self. This development, because it means that the self must be willing to suffer for something it values more than its own ease, can be one of the moving and beautiful events of a human life — it can be heroic. At any rate, the conflict between these two tendencies of the mind is at the center of all Miss McCarthy's novels. Because this conflict is her own, her reports on it have the variety, complexity, and intensity of personal experience. But because the freedom to live by ideas, ideas which may lead away from the real as well as toward it, is what distinguishes the whole class of twentieth-century intellectuals, her tales of the troubled Mary McCarthy heroine have developed naturally into social satire.

The exquisitely written *Memories of a Catholic Girlhood* (1957) reveals how deeply rooted Miss McCarthy's stories are in her own life. She tells us that she was born in Seattle in 1912 to a Protestant mother, whose own mother was Jewish and who accepted her husband's religion, and a Catholic father. The mother was beautiful. The father was a partial invalid, irresponsible as a breadwinner, but handsome, charming, a delight to his children with his stories and presents. When she was six both parents died in one week from flu. The rich McCarthy grandparents, whose Catholicism was a "sour and baleful doctrine in which old hates and rancors had been stewing for generations, with ignorance proudly stirring the pot," placed her and her three brothers in a house as poor as their own was luxurious and under the guardianship of a couple of Dickensian monsters, a great-aunt and a German-American husband. The theme of the first chapters of *Memories* is injustice, and Miss McCarthy describes the needless poverty, the ugliness, the sadistic, self-righteous beatings with an unaccustomed, if controlled, intensity of rage and pity.

At the age of eleven she was rescued and taken to Seattle by her other grandfather, also rich, but a model of the Protestant virtues. To cite qualities she later found he shared with Julius Caesar, Grandfather Preston was "just, laconic, severe, magnanimous, detached." She was no longer wretched, but she remained an outsider —in her new home, whose moral standards were oppressively high; in the Catholic convent school she went to first, where she lost her faith; later in a public school, among the school "hearties"; finally in an Episcopal boarding school, where she was set apart by her "brilliance" and her independence. And here, at sixteen, she underwent experiences which, as described in the chapter of *Memories* called "The Figures in the Clock," clearly foreshadow the characteristic moral vision, and even the organizing "conflicts," of the fiction to come.

In this chapter it is a conflict between the wicked conspirator Catiline and Julius Caesar. Acting the part of Catiline in a play written by her Latin teacher, she made a sensation by reading her lines so as to *vindicate* the rebel, to champion his self-willed brilliance — and thereby her own — against mere dull law and order. Shortly after this, however, a strange thing happened. Under the guidance of Miss Gowrie (the fictitious name she gives her teacher), the girl fell in love with Julius Caesar! "The sensation was utterly confounding. All my previous crushes had been products of my will, constructs of my personal convention, or projections of myself, the way Catiline was. This came from without and seized me . . . the first piercing contact with an impersonal reality happened to me through Caesar." She and her teacher loved that mind "immersed in practical life as in some ingenious detective novel, that wished always to show you how anything was done and under what disadvantages . . . the spirit of justice and scientific inquiry that reigned over the *Commentaries*." "Justice, good will, moderation, and *uncommon fidelity*," why, she asks, quoting Caesar's praise of a conquered Gaul loyal to himself, "should these substantives of virtue have stirred the Seminary's Catiline? At the time I was sublimely unaware that my fortifications had been breached, that the forces of law and order were pacifying the city while the rebel standard still waved on the ramparts."

What she loved in Caesar hints not only at the moral values in the novels to come, but at their art — their way with details and their way with sentences. But we are not done with the meaning of this rich chapter. Another insight alternates with the first "like the two little wooden weather figures in a German clock, one of which steps out as the other swings back into the works, in response to atmospheric pressures." The "good Gaul" whose loyalty to Caesar she and Miss Gowrie admired was after all a "quisling," traitorously loyal to his people's conqueror. Later, when "bad Gauls" merged in her mind with those who resisted Hitler, she was angry with her Latin teacher for having steered her wrong. But then, later still, it came to her that it had been Miss Gowrie who had seen to it that her Catiline costume was especially gorgeous — she has at last "an eerie sense that Miss Gowrie, unsuspected by me, was my co-conspirator." It appears that for her teacher too that preference for Caesar, for "impersonal reality" and law and order over the lawless ego, was haunted by the contradictory possibility that the ego can have a self-justifying beauty, or that law and order, with changes in "atmospheric pressure," that is, in the context, may serve error, and the self-asserting individual be in the right. And in her note to the chapter Miss McCarthy tells us that this conflict is rooted in her inheritance. "Caesar, of course, was my [Preston] grandfather . . . Catiline was my McCarthy ancestors . . . To my surprise, I chose Caesar and the rule of law. This does not mean that the seesaw between these two opposed forces terminated; one might say, in fact, that it only began during my last years in the Seminary when I recognized the beauty of an ablative absolute and of a rigorous code of conduct."

A word about her life after the Seminary. For a summer she studied acting; then, from 1929 to 1933, she attended Vassar College. In 1933 she married the actor and unsuccessful playwright Harold Johnsrud, and began to write reviews for the *New Republic* and the *Nation*. Her essay "My Confession" tells how at this time she was drawn into political controversy by her indignation at the smug dishonesty of American Communists and especially by their defense of the "Moscow trials," in which the exiled Trotsky was being discredited by an elaborate structure of lies. In 1936, her marriage dissolved, she lived in Greenwich Village, wrote reviews, and worked for an art dealer. A year later she began to write a monthly "Theater Chronicle" for the recently revived *Partisan Review*. In these essays there was much good sense and some affected and excessive rigidity of principle, as she herself admits in a preface to the book *Sights and Spectacles* (1956) in which they were later collected. In 1938 she married the critic Edmund Wilson.

The marriage ended after seven years, but he was the father of her only child Reuel, and it was at Wilson's suggestion that she began to write fiction. Her first story, "Cruel and Barbarous Treatment," became the opening chapter of *The Company She Keeps*. For two years she was a college teacher — at Bard in 1945–46 and at Sarah Lawrence in 1948–49 — and her history since then, aside from her marriage to Bowden Broadwater, which lasted from 1946 to 1961, and to James West in 1961, is mainly the history of her books.

In 1956, along with *Sights and Spectacles*, she published the first of two works on Italian cities, *Venice Observed*, and in 1959 the second, *The Stones of Florence*. Each book is an account of the city's history, architecture, art, and people. The first is the slighter, the more personal and anecdotal, the second the more sober and scholarly, and at the same time the more passionate: The art and architecture of Florence moved her intensely. This latter book, in fact, is surprisingly readable for so scholarly a work, and the reason is only in part the lively, taut, and elegant style. Even more important is her clear concern throughout with the "human interest" of the history and the art.

In 1962 the essays she had been writing since 1946 on a variety of subjects were collected in the volume *On the Contrary*. These differ in quality. Most valuable are her contributions to the political debates of the time — on the Moscow trials, on McCarthyism, on Communists in the schools — and her essays on fiction and drama, "Settling the Colonel's Hash," "The Fact in Fiction," "Characters in Fiction," and "The American Realist Playwrights." Of the latter group it is enough to say here that they constitute, by implication, a defense of the kind of art she herself has practiced. This is a realistic art, which gives us what might usefully be called *samples* of reality rather than *symbols* of it. (She herself speaks of "natural symbolism.") For the reader to do justice to such work, he needs to be alert rather to human matters — the psychological or moral meaning of actions or tones — than to literary allusions and strategies.

We are now ready for the novels, on which her permanent reputation will surely rest. The first of these, *The Company She Keeps* (1942), consists of six chapters published originally as stories in magazines. In a very interesting and useful *Paris Review* interview, Miss McCarthy has said that though she had originally intended them as separate stories, "about halfway through I began to think of them as a kind of unified story. The same character kept reappearing, and so on. I decided finally to call it a novel in that it does in a sense tell *a* story, one story." The reappearing character is Margaret Sargent, of whom we learn at the end that she was the daughter of a tolerant, intelligent Protestant father and a beautiful Catholic mother, and was brought up as a Catholic, after her mother's early death, by a vulgar and bigoted Catholic aunt. Not only has Miss McCarthy given her heroine a background substantially like her own; she has told us herself that the stories are all autobiographical except one, "Portrait of the Intellectual as a Yale Man." In fact, the book is remarkable for the honesty of its self-exposure, an exposure which dares to include the ignoble and the humiliating and which shows a kind of reckless passion for the truth that is to remain an important element of her talent.

This passion for the truth not only provides the motive power behind the self-exposure in these tales. It turns out to be their underlying subject as well. The author has suggested, and it has been repeated by many critics, that the "one story" of the book is that of the heroine's vain search, amid her many identities, for some real identity underlying them all. But this search seems actually to be less important than her moral development, a development of which the ultimate goal is not to know what she is but to behave as an adult should. What we mainly watch as her story unfolds is Miss Sargent's increasingly desperate struggle, against all the temptations to falsehood in the intellectual life of her time, to stop lying and to live by the truth.

She begins far enough from any truth. In the first chapter, "Cruel and Barbarous Treatment," which is not so much a story as a witty satire on nameless generalized types and their typical behavior, she is a married "Woman With a Secret" delighting in an affair with a "Young Man" chiefly because it "was an opportunity, unparalleled in her experience, for exercising feelings of superiority over others." Play-acting irresponsibly with life's realities, she reduces them to fashionable clichés that minister to her vanity. The second chapter, "Rogue's Gallery," in which Miss Sargent works for a rogue who runs an art gallery and appears as a naive, good-natured foil for her colorful con man of a boss, seems a mere exercise in the Dickensian picturesque. But in the third the book's deeper story continues: the heroine's play-acting is complicated by an opposing impulse. "The Man in the Brooks Brothers Shirt" is an account of how Miss Sargent, now seen in the role of poised, sophisticated New York intellectual, is drawn into an affair with a businessman on a cross-country train trip because she enjoys playing that role before such an audience. And yet, showing off an advance copy of a new book, she wonders uneasily "if her whole way of life had been assumed for purposes of ostentation." When the man speaks shrewdly about her past, she leans forward. "Perhaps at last she had found him, the one she kept looking for, the one who could tell her what she was really like. . . . If she once knew, she had no doubt that she could behave perfectly." Then there is her horrified shame, when she awakens in his compartment, at the drunken sex of the night before which she gradually remembers. (This is the first of those cool "shocking" notations of the unattractive particulars of "romantic" episodes for which Miss McCarthy has won a certain notoriety, though far from being exploitations of sex, they seem expressions of a puritanical disgust.)

15

Finally, she becomes aware of a reluctance to leave the man, who, falling in love with her, had changed in her eyes from the vulgar businessman type to an actual and attractive person; and at this "a pang of joy went through her as she examined her own sorrow and found it to be real." The affair dies away after the trip, and the story ends with both falling back into the stereotypes from which they had briefly emerged, but Margaret Sargent has acquired substance as a character with the disclosure that she is divided, like the rest of us, and that the hunger of her intellectual's vanity is opposed by a hunger for reality.

In "The Genial Host" we see this new Miss Sargent again. She is now the dinner guest of one Pflaumen, who is shown as having repressed both his natural tendency to fat and hairiness and his natural personality of a Jewish paterfamilias to become the elegant familiar and host of clever, fashionable, successful people. Moreover, this reality-avoider collects his guests for their "allegorical possibilities," that is, for the chic intellectual positions to which they have sacrificed their own reality. Thus, Margaret, hotly defending Trotsky against the party's Stalinist, and delighted at the effect she is making, is horrified to note that Pflaumen is beaming at her for performing as expected, while the party's one honest man, a poor young Jewish lawyer, is applauding ironically. The story ends in another capitulation: she dare not yet rebel against Pflaumen and the falsenesses by which she sings for her suppers, she is still too "poor, loverless, lonely." But in the next, "Portrait of the Intellectual as a Yale Man," though she is still in need, she has ceased to capitulate.

This story is mainly about the Yale Man, who, though naive and second rate, has been welcomed onto the Stalinist-dominated weekly magazine the *Liberal* because he comes as a healthy, happy, clean-cut, average American, a type rare among them. This was a time — the thirties — when out of loyalty to the ideal of communism a large proportion of the intellectual establishment had accepted so many of the lies and brutalities of the Stalin dictatorship that they had lost the sense of the relevance to politics, and even to life, of the ordinary decencies. Such people lied in defense of the Communist party's shifts in policy or vilified the opposition rather than debate with it, and did both with a sincere feeling of virtue. Jim Barnett, the Yale Man, is not one of these; he tries to be honest, but he is able to make a living as a radical political commentator only because his shallowness is precisely suited to the intellectual climate of this milieu, from which the Stalinists have largely excluded reality.

Margaret Sargent was put into this story, says Miss McCarthy, "because she had to be in it," that is, for the sake of the unity of the book to come, but her role turns out to be crucial, for she is there as an eruption of integrity into that world of blur and lies. Now when she defends Trotsky, it is among Stalinist editors who can fire her from the magazine job she needs. "You had to admire her courage," Jim thinks, "for undertaking something that cost her so much." Even her way of taking Jim for a lover is significantly different from her past behavior. She submits to this married man's sudden overpowering lust — and perhaps to her own as well — with a "disconsolate smile" — no play-acting here. Jim quits his job indignantly when she is fired, and in this time of proud excitement, he gets an idea for an important book. But the effort to write the book and to live on that moral peak is really beyond his means. He gives up both, gets a handsome job on the conservative magazine *Destiny*, and though he continues to send checks to the American Civil Liberties Union, he grows increasingly impatient with opinionated unsuccessful left-wing intellectuals. And for Margaret he comes to feel a kind of hatred. Pathetic though she is in her "too tense" clinging to her truth, in her unsuccess, she is somehow triumphant. In the story's beautifully written last pages she haunts him as a reminder of the dead illusion of his youth, the illusion that he could be free of "the cage of his own nature" and better than himself.

In the last story "Ghostly Father, I Confess," after five years of an unhappy second marriage to an architect apparently congenial but really authoritarian and unimaginative, Margaret is spending an hour on a psychoanalyst's couch. She has been sent by her husband, who is fed up with the way she uses her "wonderful scruples as an excuse for acting like a bitch." And now, though she disapproves of psychoanalysis, whose conclusions can never be proved wrong since all disagreement is mere resistance, and considers her doctor a limited man, she finds herself drawn into an agonizing search for the cause of her misery and bad behavior, for it is also a search for the "meaning" that will redeem her life from "gibberish." The story is crammed with the up-welling, emotion-charged facts of her life—from the childhood passed between her father's rationalism and her aunt's vulgarities to the second marriage, in which she feels herself suffocating amid such stylish middle-class culture-objects as "her white pots of ivy, her Venetian blinds, her open copy of a novel by Kafka. . . . each in its own patina of social anxiety." Miss McCarthy seems to have thrown boldly into the story the whole confusion of her own life. Yet it moves with a nightmarish coherence amid the chaos, and, in fact, what she understands at the end makes the story a unity and a fitting conclusion to the book's whole development.

The story is about the pressure on Margaret Sargent to accept the life of the intellectually sophisticated middle class which she detests. And for that life she is now to be made fit by a mode of "therapy" which is presented as the most insidious of all its ways of avoiding reality. The object of the therapy is to perform a "perfectly simple little operation." First the consciousness is put to sleep by "the sweet, optimistic laughing-gas of science (you are not bad, you are merely unhappy . . . poor Hitler is a paranoiac, and that dirty fornication in a hotel room, why, that, dear Miss Sargent, is a 'relationship')." Then the doctor cuts out "the festering conscience, which was of no use to you at all, and was only making you suffer." But to have a conscience is to remain aware of what is outside one's own wishes, that is, of a difference between truth, however painful, and lies, however gratifying. Under the pressure of the idea that she is unhappy merely because she is ill, "her own sense of truth was weakening. This and her wonderful scruples were all she had in the world, and they were slipping away." And it is this that makes her most miserable. She can't behave as she should, but not to know when she does evil, and not to mind, is to lose her grip on reality and to shrink from a healthy adult into an invalid or a child.

The story ends with an apparent inconclusiveness that is really, as I have said, a sufficient conclusion, both to the story and the book. She is almost persuaded by her doctor that she can be good and free and strong inside her marriage, which is to say, that all can yet be well at no painful cost, when she remembers a dream she had begun to tell him earlier. In this dream she had enabled herself to accept the embraces of a Nazi type by pretending that he was really rather Byronic. As she walks away from the doctor's office, feeling the hateful expected tug of an attraction to him, she suddenly understands the dream. It has told her that all will *not* be well, that unable to love herself except through the love of men, she will again seek a new love to rescue her from past failures and will again snatch at it blindly and perhaps unscrupulously. But though in the dream she pretended the Nazi was a Byron, "she could still detect her own frauds. At the end of the dream, her eyes were closed, but the inner eye had remained alert. . . . 'Oh my God,' she said . . . 'do not let them take this away from me. If the flesh must be blind, let the spirit see. Preserve me in disunity.'"

19

Thus is completed the "one story" of Margaret Sargent. Beginning as a manipulator and falsifier of reality, she is now its true lover, who would rather suffer than pretend and whose suffering, because it means the clarity of mind to see the truth and the courage to face it, is the measure of a new dignity.

It is no doubt true, as Elizabeth Hardwick has suggested, that all such "frank" confession is in part self-exculpation. But Miss McCarthy's frankness in confessing weakness and error in this book seems to earn her the right to move on, for a completer truth indeed, to the virtues of her defects. At any rate, the portrait of Margaret Sargent carries conviction, and her struggle toward honesty has a permanent relevance to our experience.

Certain themes in the first book are repeated in *Cast a Cold Eye* (1950), a collection of four stories and three early versions of chapters of her *Memories*. In "The Weeds" is treated somberly, and in "The Friend of the Family" with bitter humor, the sort of marriage seen in "Ghostly Father." It is the marriage that destroys the individual's integrity, his troublesome loyalty to the truth of his own nature. "The Old Men," less successful than the other two but interesting for its meanings, tells how a young man who has long been uncertain of his own identity comes to feel that the self is no more than a *"point du depart"* for "impersonations," and that reality, the actual, is "pornography" and to be avoided. At this, "blithe and ready to live, selfishly and inconsiderately," he sings out the Yeats epitaph which gives the book its title, and shortly afterward, as if for want of any reason to live, he abruptly dies. It thus appears that the "cold eye" which reviewers have generally supposed the author meant as her own is meant in fact to describe what she most reprobates, that indifference to what is outside the self which deprives the self of reality and makes life pointless.

Miss McCarthy has defended *The Oasis* (1949) from the charge that it is not a novel by insisting that it was not intended to be, that it is a *conte philosophique*. This explains its lack of action, for instead of plot we have slight episodes explored for their large meanings and characters revealed less by what they do than in long satirical descriptions. But it cannot eliminate the sense that the tale's developments, which ought after all to arise by an inner necessity, are sometimes arbitrarily asserted, as if to get things moving. And yet the reminder of an elegant eighteenth-century prose form does point to qualities that will keep the tale, in spite of its imperfections, interesting for a long time. The satirical descriptions do not merely imitate but genuinely duplicate the qualities of eighteenth-century prose masters — the psychological insight, the general wisdom, the witty, epigrammatic, gracefully balanced sentences.

The Oasis is the story of a group of New York intellectuals — based apparently on well-known friends of the author, but to the rest of us quite recognizable as contemporary types — who, shortly after World War II, form a colony called Utopia in the Taconic Mountains of New York State. The colonists fall mainly into two factions. The "purists" hope the colony will illustrate "certain notions of justice, freedom, and sociability" derived from their Founder, a saintly Italian anarchist lost in "a darkened city of Europe." This group is led by Macdougal Macdermott, a man who rightly senses that he does not naturally belong to "that world of the spirit" which he yearns to enter, but who, "ten years before . . . had made the leap into faith and sacrificed $20,000 a year and a secure career as a paid journalist for the intangible values that eluded his empirical grasp. He had moved down town into Bohemia, painted his walls indigo, dropped the use of capital letters and the practice of wearing a vest" and become the editor of a "libertarian magazine." The "realists," on the other hand, have come only for a holiday from the pressures of real life. They look upon "conspicuous goodness" like the Founder's as a "form of simple-mindedness on a par with vegetarianism, and would have refused admission to Heaven on the ground that it was full of green-horns and cranks." Moreover, they find absurd the assumption of "human freedom" which underlies all that the purists believe, for they are inheritors of Marxian "scientific socialism," and though they had discarded the dialectic and repudiated the Russian Revolution, "the right of a human being to *think* that he could resist history, environment, class structure, psychic conditioning was something they denied him with all the ferocity of their own pent-up natures and disappointed hopes." And since "ideological supremacy" has become "essential to their existence," they look forward with pleasure to the colony's failure. They do, however, wish it to fail convincingly, of its own foolishness, and this seduces them into unusually good behavior. Soon Will Taub, their leader, finds that he participates "in the forms of equity with increasing confidence, and though of course he did not take any of it *seriously*, his heavy and rather lowering nature performed the unaccustomed libertarian movements with a feeling of real sprightliness and wondering self-admiration, as if he had been learning to dance."

In Will Taub we have the first full-fledged example of the enemy in Miss McCarthy's world, the Other to all that she values. He is one who is at home only in the realm of ideas, who is flat-footed in his behavior with children, women — in all non-intellectual relations — who feels pain at the very word "Jew" because "his Jewishness [was] a thing about himself which he was powerless to alter and which seemed to reduce him therefore to a curious dependency on the given." And this rejection of the "given," the real, on behalf of a world of ideas where he can reign supreme involves too a rejection of moral responsibility. It is for the realists a felt oddity in Utopia that "here they were answerable for their deeds to someone and not simply to an historical process." And

22

Taub is even capable, like the later Henry Mulcahy, of beginning to believe his own lie (that an embarrassingly cowardly reaction of his is due to former police persecution) in order to maintain his cherished supremacy.

These two characters, and Joe Lockman, the go-getting businessman who comes to Utopia determined to get more spiritual profit out of it than anyone else, are the tale's most vivid portraits. But it is a fourth, Katy Norell, to whom its chief events tend to happen and out of whose responses its meanings emerge. Katy, a teacher of Greek, suffers from "a strong will and a weak character," an awkward compulsion to tell the truth even when it aggravates her problems, and a readiness to feel guilty when things go wrong. Though it was her "instinctive opinion . . . that the past could be altered and actions, like words, 'taken back,'" her husband's disgust with her, on one occasion when it seems serious, gives her a frightening glimpse of life "as a black chain of consequence, in which nothing was lost, forgot, forgiven, redeemed, in which the past was permanent and the present slipping away from her." This character, weak but scrupulous, who wishes life were easy but can't shut out the perception that it is hard, is, of course, a sister of Margaret Sargent as well as of the later Martha Sinnott, though, unlike the others, she pays for representing her author's inner life by being one of the less vivid characters in her book. But it is out of her inner contradictions that the book's closing insights come. These insights are initiated by the last of several challenges to the colony's "sociability" — the stealing of their strawberries by some rough interlopers, whom Katy herself, frightened when her pleading is answered with threatening gestures, demands be ejected by force. Taub taunts her with her contradiction, her yielding to "human nature," and at this, lulled or liberated by the dinner wine, she begins to understand. They did wrong, she thinks, to cling to the strawberries without needing them — it was only the idea of the strawberries they really cared about. They had let "mental images" possess them as the idea of sex dominates the mind in pornography. But the mind should stick to its own objects, "love, formal beauty, virtue"; they should not have tried to make real things dance to the mind's tune. And this is only a small example of their fundamental error. As the tale draws to an end, she realizes that Utopia is going to fail because of their wish to "*embody* virtue." If they had been content to manufacture, not virtue, but furniture, it might have survived.

It is a rueful, if not tragic, conclusion. To replace the stubborn complexity of people and society with ideas is the mistake of both parties in Utopia. The cynics who insist that our behavior is determined by history and the "idealists" who believe so easily that man can be what he wishes to be are shown to be equally removed from the life we actually live. And yet those like Katy Norell, who see through this error, who feel and suffer life up close, are better off, if at all, only because it is better to understand. For their superiority consists mainly in desiring a virtue they know they can never attain.

"And search for truth amid the groves of academe" — this quotation from Horace prefaces Miss McCarthy's next novel. The search for truth, and the human defects that hinder it, we have seen to be her permanent subject. Now again the private concern becomes a way of understanding the large public matters that her life has brought before her: this time the political liberalism of the "witch-hunting" era of Joseph McCarthy (the 1950's), when the reactionary right, not the Communist left, frightened or confused intellectuals into self-betrayal; and progressive education, with its own less obvious hindrances to the search for truth. But *The Groves of Academe* (1952) is her first real or completely successful novel because now, for the first time, she has found a setting, characters, and a plot that dramatize both her private and her public subjects in

24

one lively story. With this novel, moreover, her resemblance to Jane Austen, already evident in the irony, sanity, and grace of her prose, and the combination of moral concern and tough intelligence in her approach to people, grows even more striking. She gives us now, in that same prose, a group of characters vividly and comically idiosyncratic, with a wonderful comic villain in the center. She gives us a plot which evolves with perfect illuminating logic from the moral qualities of the characters. And she gives us the peculiarly Austenish pleasure of watching good, intelligent, and articulate people work their way through much painful error to the relief of shared understanding.

The plot is a most ingenious stroke of wit. Its humor is based on the fact that where in the outside, non-intellectual world it had become dangerous in this period to have once been a Communist, in the world of liberal intellectuals a man persecuted for a Communist past has become almost a holy martyr and entitled to defense. Miss McCarthy's joke is that when the incompetent, irresponsible (though learned and brilliant) Henry Mulcahy is about to be let go by the liberal president of Jocelyn College, he is able to win the support of his colleagues by pretending to have *been* a Communist. The joke reaches its climax when an old anarchist acquaintance of Mulcahy's is interrogated by President Hoar and a faculty committee about whether their colleague really had this claim on their respect and protection, and the anarchist, who "sings," betrays the shocking secret that Mulcahy's Communist past had been a lie. Upon which, in an explosion of topsy-turveyness, Mulcahy comes raging to Hoar like the righteous victim of a witch-hunt, and using the secret investigation as evidence that the president has betrayed his liberal principles, forces *him* to resign.

It is a pity to tell the punch line of such a story, but the fault is less grave than it might be because the fun here lies in the characters and in the fine detail by which they and their world are kept always very much alive. Most of all the story belongs to the magnificently repulsive Henry Mulcahy, in whom the kind of intellectual dishonor which we have already begun to recognize as Miss McCarthy's chief target is carried to breathtaking extremes. It is moreover a special triumph of the book that she has shown us this comic monster from the inside (she calls the technique "ventriloquism," as George Henry Lewes once wrote of Jane Austen's "dramatic ventriloquism"), mimicking his mode of thought so fully and felicitously that it is impossible, for all his excesses, not to recognize him as real.

In Henry Mulcahy, a pear-shaped, soft-bellied father of four, Ph.D., contributor to serious magazines, Guggenheim Fellow, etc., the intellectual's besetting sins — his lust for supremacy and his preference for flattering ideas over mere facts — undergo a marvelous efflorescence. He not only identifies himself with Joyce, Kafka, and other "sacred untouchables of the modern martyrology"; he comes to regard disloyalty to himself as "apostasy," and the dismayed Domna Rejnev discovers that "behind Joyce . . . is the identification with Christ." At the same time his great lie is to him the work of an artist, who creates out of life's raw material "a figurative truth more true than the data of reality." (Remembering vaguely that he had once heard the phrase "heart murmur" used of someone in his family, he is soon exclaiming to himself — sincerely! — that he holds Hoar "personally responsible for the life of his wife and/or son.") And when the defeated president finally asks him, "Are you a conscious liar or a self-deluded hypocrite?" Mulcahy replies, "A Cretan says, all Cretans are liars." Having thus put in question the very possibility of finding truth, he frankly declares, "I'm not concerned with truth. . . . I'm concerned with justice."

The faculty for whom Mulcahy has thus set a special problem in truth-seeking are all sharply realized, but those who share the center of the stage with Mulcahy are two teachers who are most different from him, and who bring what Miss McCarthy honors as effectively to life as he re-creates what she despises. Domna Rejnev and John Bentkoop are also intellectuals but to them the truth matters more than their own success and comfort. In Miss Rejnev, beautiful twenty-three-year-old daughter of Russian emigrés, whose "finely cut, mobile nostrils quivered during a banal conversation as though, literally, seeking air," and who, in a crisis, asks herself "What would Tolstoy say?" this intellectual passion is endearingly childlike in its ardor and even in its vanity. The ardor we see when she hears of Mulcahy's "persecution": "Her strange, intent eyes were shining; she tossed her head angrily and the dark, clean hair bobbed; she clicked her pocket-lighter and drew in on a cigarette. 'This cannot be permitted to happen,' she declared quickly, amid puffs of smoke. 'One simply refuses it and tells Maynard Hoar so.' She jumped up, knocking a book off the desk, and seized her polo coat from the coatrack. 'I shall do it myself at once to set an example.' "

And we see the vanity when she warmly praises Mulcahy's learning to silent colleagues out of her pleasure in honoring excellence. "She rather enjoyed the idea that she was sufficiently spendthrift (that is, sufficiently rich in resources)." But this pride is so far from the smug confidence of the self-worshippers that a colleague lets her pour out a passionate argument without interrupting "because he knew her to be honest and presumed that therefore, before she had finished, a doubt would suddenly dart out of her like a mouse from its hole." Sure enough, it is her agonizing recognition not only that she had been wrong about Mulcahy, but that she had been seduced into pretending not to know defects in him which she did know, into a sort of lying, that is to be her climactic experience in the book.

The deep, the metaphysical opposition between Mulcahy's kind and hers emerges during a painful dinner at the Mulcahy home when Domna suddenly learns she has been defending a liar. Uneasy, he tries to recoup by suggesting that, being handsome, she is a "monist," but that unattractive people like himself "know that appearances are fickle. We look to somebody else to discover our imperishable essence." And he asks her if she could love a leper, meaning, as she understands, himself. "If you mean a moral leper, no," she says. "Fair without and foul within has no charm for me. Nor the reverse, for that matter. . . . People whose inside contradicts their outside . . . have neither essence nor existence." Mulcahy, in short, can feel virtuous when he does evil and entitled to loyalty even by those whom he betrays because he believes instinctively in a sort of dualism according to which the concrete world, where actions have consequences and entail responsibilities, can be regarded as mere "appearance" — of secondary importance beside those abstractions (Norine Schmittlapp of *The Group* will call them "intangibles") which his ego can manipulate. The others are like Domna — or like Virginia Bentkoop, who, in a charming touch, though "she had met Domna only once, at a college lecture . . . divined correctly that her feet were wet." They are people who notice and respect the actualities of the world.

This, however, is a progressive college, and these are liberals of the fifties, and the combination has guaranteed Mulcahy's triumph. For, as the novel has also been suggesting, and as one teacher puts it at the end, progressive education means a concern with "faith and individual salvation" — that is, the student's inner quality is considered to be more important than his demonstrated mastery, through hard work, of real subject matter. This has a sinister resemblance to Mulcahy's self-defense that "appearance" — the mere concrete facts of what one is and does — is somehow less important than one's invisible "essence." And it is a view that is plainly akin to the tendency of many liberals of the era to separate "justice," in the words of Mulcahy again, from "truth," to consider scruples that interfered with work for a "good cause" mere ivory tower pedantry. Not that Miss McCarthy fails to make clear that the progressive college and its liberal faculty are right and attractive in many ways, and create a world in which good things can grow as well as bad. But her story makes it even clearer that there is no safety in good intentions when their pursuit requires us to ignore the truth.

Because *The Groves of Academe* is about college teachers, much of its drama comes to us in the clash of explicit ideas amid explicit descriptions of the college world and its intellectual character. For some readers this may sometimes clog or confuse the otherwise lively story. There can be no such objection to *A Charmed Life* (1955), for though this novel is equally rich in meaning, its meaning is more centrally human and expressed more completely by the rushing story alone. And the style, having to argue and explain less, having only to serve the urgent events and emotions, seems lighter, swifter, and richer in Miss McCarthy's characteristic poetry.

Perhaps too the novel is her best so far, the most poignant and powerful under the usual ironic control, because she has here found a subject which dramatizes the conflict among her own most cherished values — that "seesaw" between the demands of the self and those of "impersonal reality" — and which therefore taps her own strongest feelings. This conflict is foreshadowed in a new twist given to her familiar heroine. Martha Sinnott is another woman of mind, another lover of that "impersonal reality," but an element in the type hitherto regarded as only a source of difficulty is now permitted to present fully its own case. For this very clever and learned young playwright is also a woman, as her husband tells us, with "an obstinate childish heart," one to whom reality speaks a "little language" and who cannot bear that it ever utter, in her marriage, what is not true and beautiful and good. She not only insists that life conform to her dream, but, to make it conform, she dares to act as if, in the words of Katy Norell in her weakness, "the past could be altered and actions, like words, 'taken back.' " Miss McCarthy herself tells us that the novel is about "doubt," and it is true that the doubt which, among contemporary intellectuals, automatically dogs every dream and every piety is important in the story. But even more important is the "obstinate childish heart" by which the doubt is opposed. It is her heroine's "romanticism" that is now this "neoclassic" novelist's subject, and it is that romanticism's tormenting ambiguity which gives the story its wealth of meaning and its almost desperate intensity.

The romantic demand which Martha Sinnott (her last name suggests the McCarthy heroine's usual vain wish) makes upon life acquires a special urgency as the story opens because she has, to finish a play, come back with her second husband to the same Cape Cod town where she had once lived with her first — that is, to a place where her new love and new hope are in danger. New Leeds is dangerous for two reasons. First, because it is a contemporary Bohemia, full of artists and intellectuals who live in a state of freedom from tradition, convention, morality, and regular work. These are people who are always divorcing and remarrying, sinking into alcoholism or fighting it, falling down flights of stairs or into wells, and who yet seem to bear a charmed life — nothing seems to hurt them. The reason for this grows clear when Martha, in a moment of near hysteria, cries out that though the New Leedsian will never "admit to knowing anything, until it's been proved," and though he is always setting himself free to do as he pleases by demanding, "Explain to me why not. Give me one reason why not," the fact is, "you don't really doubt. You just ask questions, like a machine. . . . Nobody is really curious because nobody cares what the truth is." The New Leedsian's life is charmed into unreality by his moral indifference. Nothing really matters to him and so nothing can really hurt him. And that she is right to fear this moral casualness emerges when her husband goes out of town for a night and she is brought together by a friend — for the fun of it — with her ex-husband Miles Murphy.

Miles is the second danger she fears. He is not quite a typical New Leedsian, since he is capable of disciplined study and work (he is a writer and a psychologist). But he shares with the others their moral qualities. He is unscrupulous, and can cheat not only an insurance company but a friend. And he is brutally self-regarding and self-assertive: Martha had never been able to resist his utter inability to doubt himself.

What all this clearly promises is fulfilled when Miles takes her home from the party. After a struggle in which she yields partly to force but even more to the pressure of Miles's conviction that it isn't worth fighting — there is no "reason why not" — she lets him have her. One reason soon appears. Shortly afterward she finds herself pregnant. And though for the ordinary New Leedsian this would not have mattered, since her husband need never know what happened, for Martha it matters to the point of anguish. She cannot bear to have a child of whose paternity she must always be in doubt, or who might give the awful Miles a claim on her, and she cannot bear to base her life with John upon a lie. She decides to have an abortion. And it is in her struggle to determine whether this is right or wrong that we come upon that ambiguity already mentioned.

Such a way of making everything beautiful again has, to begin with, an unsettling resemblance to the ordinary New Leedsian's tendency to evade the consequences of his mistakes, to shirk responsibility. And yet the romantic dream need not always be self-indulgent fantasy. It may be the faith — the religion — which

directs and ennobles our lives. In fact, Martha's inner struggle is
sometimes described in religious terms. During one terrible night
she is besieged and tempted by the devil himself, and at her blackest
hour she finds rising to her lips the cry, "Father, let this cup pass
from me." *Her* devil, of course, is a New Leedsian. "The medieval
temptations, with all the allures of gluttony and concupiscence
could not, Martha thought, have been half so trying as the sheer
dentist-drill boredom of listening to the arguments of the devil
as a modern quasi-intellectual." He utters now all the bright ideas
of contemporary sophistication, and his object is to convince her
that her vision of the good cannot stand up under rational cross-
examination. (In the voice of the psychologist Miles the devil
whispers that she doesn't really want a baby and is merely seizing
this pretext to get rid of it.)

Her dream is thus opposed by the devil because it is a dream of
living for what is right and not for what is merely pleasant. Indeed,
among her weapons, as she struggles, is a sense of how the right
makes itself known that would have won the approval of the
author of *Pilgrim's Progress*. It is worth quoting for its bold re-
capitulation of an unfashionable morality, as well as for its prose.

Yet all the while the moral part of Martha knew that she would
have to have an abortion because all her inclinations were the other
way. The hardest course was the right one; in her experience, this
was an almost invariable law. If her nature shrank from the task,
if it hid and cried piteously for mercy, that was a sign that she was
in the presence of the ethical. She knew this also from the fact that
she felt no need to seek advice; what anyone else would do under
the circumstances had no bearing. The moral part of her seemed
to square its shoulders dissociating itself from the mass of weakness that remained. It was almost a social question, she observed
with wan interest: the moral part of her would stop speaking if
she did not do what it commanded. But how, she cried out, weep-
ing. How am I to do it, all by myself? There was no answer. The
rest of her, the low part, apparently, was supposed to devise the

methods. The lawgiver was impractical, a real lady, disdaining to soil its hands, leaving the details to its servants. Martha could have laughed aloud, except for the pride and awe she felt in the acquaintance. She would not have guessed she had so much integrity. In the midst of her squirming and anguish, there was a sensation of pleased surprise.

Thus the past-canceling abortion, which might well have seemed a New Leedsian act, takes on the character of an act of moral heroism, of faith.

Having won the inner battle, she gets the external help she needs from the artist Warren Coe. Warren, a beautifully realized comic character who listens with enormous respect to the "deep" talk of people like Martha and seems created to be her butt, turns out to be her very counterpart in what matters most. What he is and what the others are and, indeed, what the whole story is about is suggested in a delightful discussion of Racine's *Bérénice* which is read aloud at that fateful New Leeds party. This play, in which the newly crowned emperor Titus must renounce forever his beloved Hebrew queen because a Roman may not marry a foreign monarch, is a tragedy about the conflict between love and duty. And though Miles and Martha came together at first like brilliant equals among ordinary people, it soon appears that it is Warren and not Miles whose ideas she shares. Miles thinks "love is for boys and women," at which Martha raises her brows and Warren, hearing his wife blandly agree, declares, "I could eat that *rug*." When Warren wants to give a hypothetical man who likes to murder old women a reason not to, Martha sympathizes with his wish for universal principles outside the self's wishes, but Miles thinks we do what we can get away with. "The electric chair . . . that's the reason we give him," he tells Warren, and then adds a remark for which one is tempted to forgive him all his crimes: "For you, it's an academic question. If you don't want to murder

33

old women, let it go at that. Don't worry about the other fellow. Live selfishly." The play itself illuminates Martha's position by contrast. It is Racine's view that one can't live the moral life and have one's heart's desire as well. But Martha wants honor *and* she wants her love, she wants both together again as if her one lapse had never occurred; and in the world of Mary McCarthy, as well as of Racine, such a wish has to be vain.

As Martha is driving home from the Coes' with Warren's loan for the abortion in her pocketbook, her husband, who thinks her recent preoccupation has been due to her worry about buying him a proper Christmas present, leaves a note in her typewriter: "Martha, I love you, but life is serious. You must not spend any money on Christmas." And in this moving touch we are surely intended to see that John is not as mistaken in the nature of her errand as he appears on the surface. She does want to buy him a present, and she is buying him something only an "obstinate childish heart," impatient of adult seriousness, would dare to fix on. Moreover, she turns out to be childishly extravagant too — she pays with her life. She is killed in a head-on collision with another car. This death has been called arbitrary, but it is, with a sort of playfulness, given roots in the tale. The other car is driven by a woman who significantly resembles Martha, a woman with a past, a writer, an intellectual, and a "cautionary example of everything Martha was trying not to be," and she is driving — of course — on the wrong side of the road. It is clearly because Martha has been such a woman that she is now at the woman's mercy. With this death, the real, with its chain of ineluctable consequences, asserts its dominion over her romantic dream.

And yet — is Martha only another New Leedsian after all? Obviously, she is not — she bears no charmed life. The saving difference is that she cares, "cares about the truth," and cares enough— Miss McCarthy tells us this in the *Paris Review* — to "put up a real stake." We read near the end, "The past *could* be undone, in certain conditions. It could be bought back, paid for by suffering. That is, it could be redeemed." In fact, what makes her happy in her last moments is the conviction that she is earning back, by means of her suffering, the right to her husband's trust, that whether or not she later tells him what she has done, her ordeal would restore "truth between them again," and "it would be all right." It is apparently thus, and thus alone, that the romantic's "obstinate childish heart" can be reconciled, in the world of Mary McCarthy, with her implacable devotion to "impersonal reality."

The Group (1963) was Miss McCarthy's first best seller, but to many critics it was an embarrassing failure. There were two main objections to the book. The first was that it exhibited a descent, surprising in so "intellectual" a writer, to the preoccupations and the language of women's magazines. The second was that its characters were "dummies," all alike and all created merely to be "humiliated." Now it is true that the success of the book is not uniform throughout, but to speak of that kind of "descent" was possible only to those who took literally what was intended as irony, who ascribed to the author preoccupations and language of which the whole point is that they testify to the limitations of the characters. (Miss McCarthy herself has said that the novel is "as far as I can go in ventriloquism," and that almost all of it is enclosed in "invisible quotation marks.") And that same inattention to significant detail probably accounts for the failure to notice that the novel's many characters are, in fact, sharply distinct from each other. The truth is, *The Group* differs from her early work mainly in its scope. Where each previous novel had been about some problem of a committed intellectual (though her heroines did indeed yearn toward the more centrally human), *The Group* is about the characteristic attitudes and life patterns of a whole social class, as shown in the loves, jobs, marriages, and housekeeping, as well as the clichés of thought and language, of a group of more or less ordinary girls.

To this one must immediately add, however, that the girls in her group *are* upper-middle-class college graduates of the thirties, which is to say they belong to a species one of whose main characteristics is a pride in keeping up with advanced ideas. In fact, these girls are a suitable subject for their author because their chief problem is another version of Miss McCarthy's permanent problem: the danger to the emotional and moral life, when the guidance of family ties and traditions has disappeared, of the freedom to live by ideas. Miss McCarthy has said the novel is about "the loss of faith in progress." This must refer to the author's own loss of such faith, since the characters who have it keep it to the end; it might be more exact to say that the novel shows the poisonous effects of that faith — of the confidence of most of these ordinary girls that they know better how to manage their lives than people ever knew before. In general, their troubles result from the fact that they are cut off by their advanced ideas from the realities of life and their own nature; less up-to-date, they might well have been better and happier people.

The novel consists of chapters written from the viewpoint and in the language of the chief members of a group of Vassar friends (class of '33), and what unifies their varied, interweaving histories is the story of one of them, Kay Strong. It is at Kay's marriage to Harald Petersen in 1933 that we first meet them, at her funeral seven years later that we see them together for the last time, and it is mainly because of her, her parties and her often grotesquely pitiful troubles, that the girls keep coming together during the years between. A sketch of what the girls are like and of what they represent should make clear both the qualities and the meaning of the novel.

Kay seems at times an oddly confused conception. Miss Mc-

Carthy apparently began by thinking of her as another "sister" to Margaret Sargent; at least, her college personality and her life seem clearly autobiographical. An attractive girl, she came to Vassar from out West, dominated her college friends with her crushing analytical cleverness, was interested in the theater, married a would-be playwright whose bullying made her miserable, longed to be admired and was often awkwardly honest. But the girl whose troubles we now follow — this later Kay quite convincing and alive — lacks any kind of intellectual distinction or even interests and could not conceivably dominate anyone. In fact, her tragedy is precisely that she is a childlike creature, "a stranger and a sojourner" in this time and place, and pathetically driven by a snobbish longing for "nice" things, who depends for her ideas and for her prospects of acquiring identity, self-respect, admiration on a husband who totally fails her. This husband is another of Miss McCarthy's fine monsters of egoism. A second-rate talent whose ambition is due mainly to jealousy of the rich and the successful and whose cheap brilliance is used for self-display, self-exculpation, or the sadistic pleasure of exercising his power over his vulnerable wife, he is shaped to be the perfect frustration of her needs. He denies, for instance, with his ill-bred, outsider's contempt for all tradition, Kay's need for traditional elegance in the home and at the table. Some funny and horrible moments come from their warring ideas of a proper meal.

Priss and Libby are simpler, less interesting types. The first is mousy and stammering, loves neatness and order, and is easily mastered by tidy theories and confident men. Seeing a stain on a friend's dress, she mentally applies Energine ("her neat little soul scrubbed away"), and it is she who is the book's ardent New Deal Democrat, eager to make society too conform to an ideal of the reasonable. (Her pediatrician husband is an anti-Roosevelt Republican, but he is infatuated with his own new deal in the form of up-to-date theories of infant care, theories he forces on his screaming baby and equally suffering wife with inhuman rigidity.) Libby, on the other hand, is not interested in bettering the world but in rising in it, her need to be the envied heroine of every encounter so frantic that she is incapable of even thinking the truth, and her chattering mouth seems to Polly like a "running wound."

With Dottie we come to a more original creation. Dottie is a shy, humorless, literal-minded girl, who is most at home in cosy chats with "Mother" and whose shyness conceals a great power of love, sexual and emotional. Her story is a tragicomedy in which a girl clearly made to be happy with old-fashioned romance and marriage but ready to behave as the new epoch thinks right is coolly and efficiently deflowered and then sent to be fitted for a pessary by a lover who doesn't even kiss her, let alone pretend that the "affair" has anything to do with love. (Docile little student of the *Zeitgeist* though she is, that omitted kiss does bother her.) Later, in one of the novel's wittiest and most touching scenes it is her *mother* who, with a timidly "bold" respect for love which is already out of date, presses Dottie to seek out that first lover. Dottie, scorning those old attitudes (and her own emotions), insists on going through with a practical marriage.

In Norine Schmittlapp Blake, occasional mistress of Kay's husband, Miss McCarthy gives us another example of that perversion of the life of the mind to which clever people are liable — this time as it appears among ordinary college graduates. Her mind and her talk are wholly given up to advanced ideas — her very apartment, painted black as Macdermott's was painted indigo, is a "dogmatic lair," all its furnishings "pontificating . . . articles of belief." She is so quick to display her superior progressiveness that it is she who announces near the end the change from one epoch and style of intellectual cliché to another by declaring that of course "No first-rate mind can accept the concept of progress any more." As

38

before in Miss McCarthy's work, the reason for such a love of "ideas" is an inability to see, let alone to value, real things, an inability that is almost literally a blindness. This was foreshadowed in college, where she declared that a Cézanne still life (which the coldly knowing Lakey called "the formal arrangement of shapes") presented "the spirit of the apples." That phrase, with its implied scorn for the concrete, becomes her *Leitmotif*, and we find her later feeling pleasantly superior to people like the sensible Helena, who seems to shrink from "imponderables" and "intangibles." (It is part of the same indictment that her husband Putnam is a fund-raiser and publicist for labor organizations, that is, not a real laborer at anything, but a manipulator of notions and "images" for causes that entitle him to feel virtuous even if he lies — and that he is impotent.) Not only is Norine's apartment so filthy that poor Helena experiences an awkward block when she goes to her bathroom; her preference for lofty "intangibles" over mere realities enables her to feel superior in virtue while she is up to her neck in moral nastiness. This is carried to a comic climax when Helena asks her pointedly where Kay had been while Norine and Kay's husband were, as Norine put it, with her fine intellectual disdain for middle-class euphemisms, "fornicating" on her couch. " 'Kay [a Macy's employee] was working,' said Norine. 'The stores don't observe Lincoln's Birthday. They cash in on the fact that the other wage slaves get the day off. It's a big white-collar shopping spree. When do you think a forty-eight-hour-week stenographer gets a chance to buy herself a dress? Unless she goes without her lunch? Probably you've never thought.' "

This extreme example of the mode of life and thought Miss McCarthy detests evokes, in one of the novel's best scenes, a wonderful explosion of the other mode by which she has always opposed it. It is Helena who explodes, the rich girl to whose parents Miss McCarthy gave her own Protestant grandfather's wealth and his passion for education, and whose encyclopedic knowledge and many accomplishments have left her wry, unassertive, good-natured — passionate about nothing but the truth. The simple concreteness of what she says when at last she can stomach Norine's falseness and ugliness no more, though it is intended literally, is also intended as samples of larger things, and her outburst is worth quoting at length because it is so funny and true and because it can be taken as implying the fundamental McCarthy creed.

". . . if I were a socialist, I would try to be a good person. . . . You say your husband can't sleep with you because you're a 'good woman.' . . . Tell him what you do with Harald. . . . That ought to get his pecker up. And have him take a look at this apartment. And at the ring around your neck. If a man slept with you, you'd leave a ring around him. Like your bathtub. . . . I'd get some toilet paper. There isn't any in the bathroom. And some Clorox for the garbage pail and the toilet bowl. And boil out that dishcloth or get a new one. . . . I'd unchain the dog and take him for a walk. And while I was at it, I'd change his name." "You don't like Nietzsche?" "No," said Helena, dryly. "I'd call him something like Rover." Norine gave her terse laugh. "I get it," she said appreciatively. "God, Helena, you're wonderful! Go on. Should I give him a bath to christen him?" Helena considered. "Not in this weather. He might catch cold. Take a bath yourself, instead . . . And buy some real food — not in cans. If it's only hamburger and fresh vegetables and oranges." Norine nodded. "Fine. But now tell me something more basic." . . . "I'd paint this room another color." . . . "Is that what you'd call basic?" she demanded. "Certainly," said Helena. "You don't want people to think you're a fascist, do you?" she added, with guile. "God, you're dead right," said Norine. "I guess I'm too close to these things. . . . Next?" "I'd take some real books out of the library." "What do you mean, 'real books'?" said Norine, with a wary glance at her shelves. [Earlier we had been told that these shelves contained "few full-size books, except for Marx's *Capital*, Pareto, Spengler, *Ten Days That Shook the World*, *Axel's Castle*, and Lincoln Steffens," all trademarks, as it were, of the radical intellectuals of the time.]

40

"Literature," retorted Helena. "Jane Austen. George Eliot. Flaubert. Lady Murasaki. Dickens. Shakespeare. Sophocles. Aristophanes. Swift." "But those aren't seminal," said Norine, frowning. "So much the better," said Helena. . . . "Is that all?" said Norine. Helena shook her head. Her eyes met Norine's. "I'd stop seeing Harald," she said.

Two members of the group remain to be mentioned, aside from fat comfortable Pokey, who is most valuable for bringing into the story her funny parents, absolutely stupefied with their wealth and self-importance, and their even funnier butler, Hatton, whose mastery of his profession entitles him to a self-importance greater, if possible, than that of his employers. These other two rank with Helena among the characters respected by their author, and with them the novel comes to an end.

Helena, Lakey, and Polly have Miss McCarthy's respect because, like other characters she has valued, they are honest, incapable of hurting or using others for their own advantage, and attentive to what is outside themselves — they notice things. But they differ significantly too. In Helena and Lakey intellectual development has crippled ordinary humanity. Helena is so enormously cultivated, so utterly knowing, that she is incapable of passion — except, as I've said, for the truth. She is cool, virginal, she even looks like a boy rather than a woman — charming to talk to, in short, but not a girl to marry. In Lakey it is her sensibility that has suffered the crippling overdevelopment. She is aware of failures of tact or artistic taste to the point, at times, of torture. It is fitting that she becomes an expatriate, spending years as a rich student and connoisseur of art in Europe, and that, though her exquisite refinement is housed, appropriately enough, in a person of exquisite beauty, she too turns out to be a girl one doesn't marry. She startles her friends by returning from Europe with a woman lover, as if, for the most scrupulous feminine sensibility, the male is too gross. This is not shown as a degradation. She is now obviously attractive as a human being, able to wince at her past snobberies, and so on. But she is also obviously incomplete. Polly Andrews alone is all that a woman ought to be, and this may be why she is referred to several times as a creature out of a fairy tale.

Polly seems, in fact, to be an audacious embodiment of a McCarthy daydream, the author's "ideal," the sort of person the little daughter of her gay invalid father and beautiful mother might have become if her hair were long and golden, if her parents had lived, and if her happy childhood had fulfilled itself, after the inevitable fairy tale trials, in a properly happy ending. For Polly's childhood too was delightful with games and presents. Her father too — one of Miss McCarthy's most successful comic creations — is a gay, fun-dispensing invalid. (He is a manic-depressive.) In her poor apartment house, Polly seems to her first lover "a girl in a story book — a fairy tale. A girl with long fair hair who lives in a special room surrounded by kindly dwarfs." What is this fairy tale creature like? She takes pleasure in the work of the kitchen, and even the laundry, she makes her own Christmas presents, she is happy and generous in love, she has a sense of humor — in short, she has the gift of being able to live enjoyably in the real world. Then, as we have found before, this openness to the real has a moral dimension. She is not only honest and morally conscientious — often to comic and troublesome extremes — she is a nurse: her profession is to help people. When she decides to marry a handsome doctor, her chief praise of him is that he is "good." (An oddly foreign word to people in her world — her mother says, "I suppose you mean he's a bit of an idealist.") And yet — her Jim is a psychiatrist. But no, this turns out to be only a spell put on him by the evil spirits of the *Zeitgeist*. He took up psychiatry, he explains, under the mistaken impression that it was a science, but he is changing to research. He will study "brain chemistry" — that is, the reader of Mary McCarthy will by now understand, he will give up the delusive freedom of psychiatry, a freedom to deal masterfully in untestable ideas, and work instead with concrete "impersonal" realities. Polly marries this good man, and taking her father to stay with them — to the horror of all their up-to-date friends — they live happily, for all we know, ever after.

As I have said, *The Group* is not perfectly successful. A defect of its method is that characters whose human importance is comparatively trifling (Libby) or who are of mainly sociological interest (Priss) are treated as fully as those who engage the author more deeply; with such characters, though they are often amusing, the narrative urgency slackens. And there are Polly's two lovers, who seem created only to make points with or to serve the plot. Nevertheless, the book is mainly a pleasure to read. The pleasure comes from the characters (most of them), so pathetic and comic, so true, in their struggle to live up to their advanced ideas or to cling to reality amid the general falsenesses; from the continuous vivifying detail of their setting, appearance, tone, and gesture; and from the sheer quantity of people and experiences the story brings to life.

Miss McCarthy has published one book since *The Group*, a collection of three articles, plus a chapter of "Solutions," called *Vietnam* (1967). This book followed a trip to Vietnam and is a report of her impressions of the war which, for eight years, the United States had been waging in that country, a war which some Americans regard as a righteous crusade against communism and others as an unwarranted, arrogant, and brutal intervention in another country's internal affairs. The book expresses the latter point of view, and gives for it an appalling and convincing mass of evidence. This is not the place to comment on her position. But what is relevant here is the intensity of her involvement in this great public tragedy, and of her insistence that it must be regarded as a moral problem, to be solved by doing not what is "practical" but what is right. "Either it is *morally* wrong for the United States to bomb a small and virtually defenseless country or it is not," she tells us, "and a student picketing the Pentagon is just as great an expert in that realm, to say the least, as Dean Rusk or Joseph Alsop." Reading this sentence — and indeed the whole book — one wonders if it is only Domna Rejnev who asks herself the question "What would Tolstoy say?"

Such undercutting of complicated authoritative theorizing by a return to the human realities which the theories obscure is, we have seen, the primary action of Miss McCarthy's mind. It is in this sense that she is a "realist," and this is why realism, which it is nowadays fashionable to consider a worked-out vein, has shown in her fiction undiminished possibilities of intelligence, feeling, wit, and grace. She herself remarks in the *Paris Review* that she can't help "a sort of distortion, a sort of writing on the bias, seeing things with a swerve and a swoop, a sort of extravagance." But though, like any serious artist, she selects her own kind of data to serve her own vision, her stories are surely offered as true examples of the experience of our time. That "swerve and swoop" are only the wit, play, and poetry in her manner of reporting what she has seen, and these qualities are not more important in her work than her accuracy. Like the "philosophy of life" it expresses, her art comes from her loyalty to the life we actually live, her pleasure in the concrete particulars of people and the world, her refusal to be seduced away from them by ideas, however fashionable or however flattering. She is, in fact, one of several current novelists and critics — Saul Bellow, with his boisterous insistence on the life of feeling, is one; Lionel Trilling, with his critique of what he calls the "second environment," that cosy conformist world of received ideas inhabited by so many "nonconformists," is another — who write out of impatience with their own class of intellectuals. Different though they are in so many ways (Bellow, for instance, quite as "romantic" as Miss McCarthy is "neoclassic"), they stand together against the intellectual's tendency to value chic ideas more than the human experience or the human ends they are supposed to serve, or, worse still, to conceal from themselves, with the help of such ideas, realities they prefer not to see.

As for the contempt thought by many to be her sole motive power, the cutting satire supposed to be her main quality, these, as I have tried to make clear, are by-products of something more fundamental. They come not from an intellectual's superciliousness but from an intellectual's hunger for the ordinary decencies and delights of life. When she strikes out, it is precisely at the kind of people who think cleverness is better. What has given Miss McCarthy's work its deepest interest is that, with all her "brilliance," she knows very well how little the mind's accomplishments may be worth in the face of life's agonizing difficulties, and that before the non-intellectual virtues — kindness, honesty, conscientiousness, the ability to take pleasure in people and the world — she lowers willingly her formidable weapons.

✦ Selected Bibliography

Works of Mary McCarthy

FICTION

The Company She Keeps. New York: Simon and Schuster, 1942.
The Oasis. New York: Random House, 1949.
Cast a Cold Eye. New York: Harcourt, Brace, and World, 1950.
The Groves of Academe. New York: Harcourt, Brace, and World, 1952.
A Charmed Life. New York: Harcourt, Brace, and World, 1955.
The Group. New York: Harcourt, Brace, and World, 1963.
"The Hounds of Summer," *New Yorker*, 30:47–50 (September 14, 1963).
"Birds of America," *Southern Review*, 1(n.s.):644–83 (July 1965).

NONFICTION

Sights and Spectacles: 1937–1956. New York: Farrar, Straus, and Company, 1956.
Venice Observed. New York: Reynal and Company, 1956.
Memories of a Catholic Girlhood. New York: Harcourt, Brace, and World, 1957.
The Stones of Florence. New York: Harcourt, Brace, and World, 1959.
On the Contrary: Articles of Belief, 1946–1961. New York: Noonday Press, 1962.
"General Macbeth," *Harper's*, 224:35–39 (June 1962).
"J. D. Salinger's Closed Circuit," *Harper's*, 205:46–48 (October 1962).
Mary McCarthy's Theatre Chronicles, 1937–1962. New York: Noonday Press, 1963.
"On Madame Bovary," *Partisan Review*, 31:174–88 (Spring 1964).
"The Inventions of I. Compton-Burnett," *Encounter*, 27:19–31 (November 1966).
Vietnam. New York: Harcourt, Brace, and World, 1967.

CURRENT AMERICAN REPRINTS

Cast a Cold Eye and *Oasis*. New York: Signet (New American Library). $.75.
A Charmed Life. New York: Signet. $.75.
The Company She Keeps. New York: Harvest (Harcourt, Brace, and World). $1.95.
The Group. New York: Signet. $.95.
The Groves of Academe. New York: Signet. $.75.
Memories of a Catholic Girlhood. New York: Berkeley. $.75.
The Stones of Florence. New York: Harvest. $1.35.
Venice Observed. New York: Harvest. $1.35.

Selected Bibliography

Bibliography

Goldman, Sherli Evens. *Mary McCarthy: A Bibliography*. New York: Harcourt, Brace, and World, 1968.

Critical and Biographical Studies

Auchincloss, Louis. "Mary McCarthy," in *Pioneers and Caretakers*. Minneapolis: University of Minnesota Press, 1965.

Brower, Brock. "Mary McCarthyism," *Esquire*, 58:62–67, 113 (July 1962).

Grumbach, Doris. *The Company She Kept*. New York: Coward-McCann, 1967.

Hardwick, Elizabeth. "Mary McCarthy," in *A View of My Own: Essays in Literature and Society*. New York: Noonday Press, 1963.

Kazin, Alfred. *Starting Out in the Thirties*. Boston: Little Brown, 1965. Pp. 155 et seq.

Mailer, Norman. "The Case against McCarthy: A Review of *The Group*," in *Cannibals and Christians*. New York: Dial Press, 1966.

McKenzie, Barbara. *Mary McCarthy*. New York: Twayne Publishers, 1966.

Niebuhr, Elisabeth. "The Art of Fiction XXVII," *Paris Review*, 27:58–94 (Winter–Spring 1962).

47